Our Place

by Anne Phillips
illustrated by Meryl Treatner

Scott Foresman

Editorial Offices: Glenview, Illinois • New York, New York
Sales Offices: Reading, Massachusetts • Duluth, Georgia
Glenview, Illinois • Carrollton, Texas • Menlo Park, California

A tree is a place for a twig.
A twig is a place for a web.
A web is a place for a spider.

Open up! Open up!
Flies for dinner!

A branch is a place for a nest.
A nest is a place for eggs.
An egg is a place for a little bird.

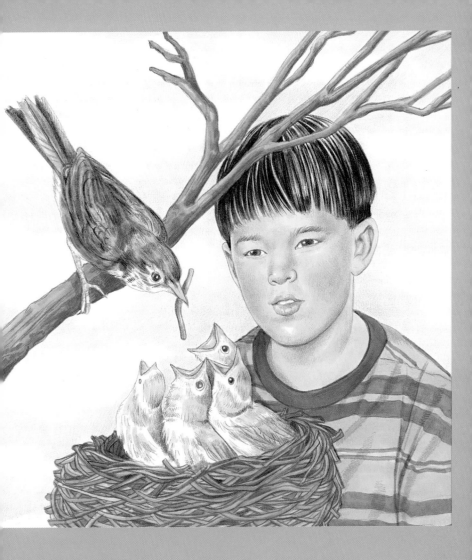

What does a little bird want?
Worms!
Open up! Open up!
Worms for dinner!

A yard is a place for a garden.
A garden is a place for a flower.
A flower is a place for a bee.

Look out!
Don't smell that flower.

A yard is a place for a bush.
A bush is a place for leaves.
The leaves are a place for a rabbit.

Come out, rabbit!
Rabbits always like carrots.
Open up! Open up!
Carrots for dinner!

A road is a place for a wall.
A wall is a place for a hole.
A hole is a place for a mouse.

Run away, mouse!
Here comes a snake!

A pond is a place for a rock.
A rock is a place for a shell.
A shell is a place for a turtle.

Oh, turtle!
Why do you always hide?

Where is a place for a yard?
Where is a place for a tree?
Where is a place for a garden?
Where is a place for a bee?

Where is a place for a pond?
Where is a place for a wall?
Where is a place for me?

Here is a place for us all.